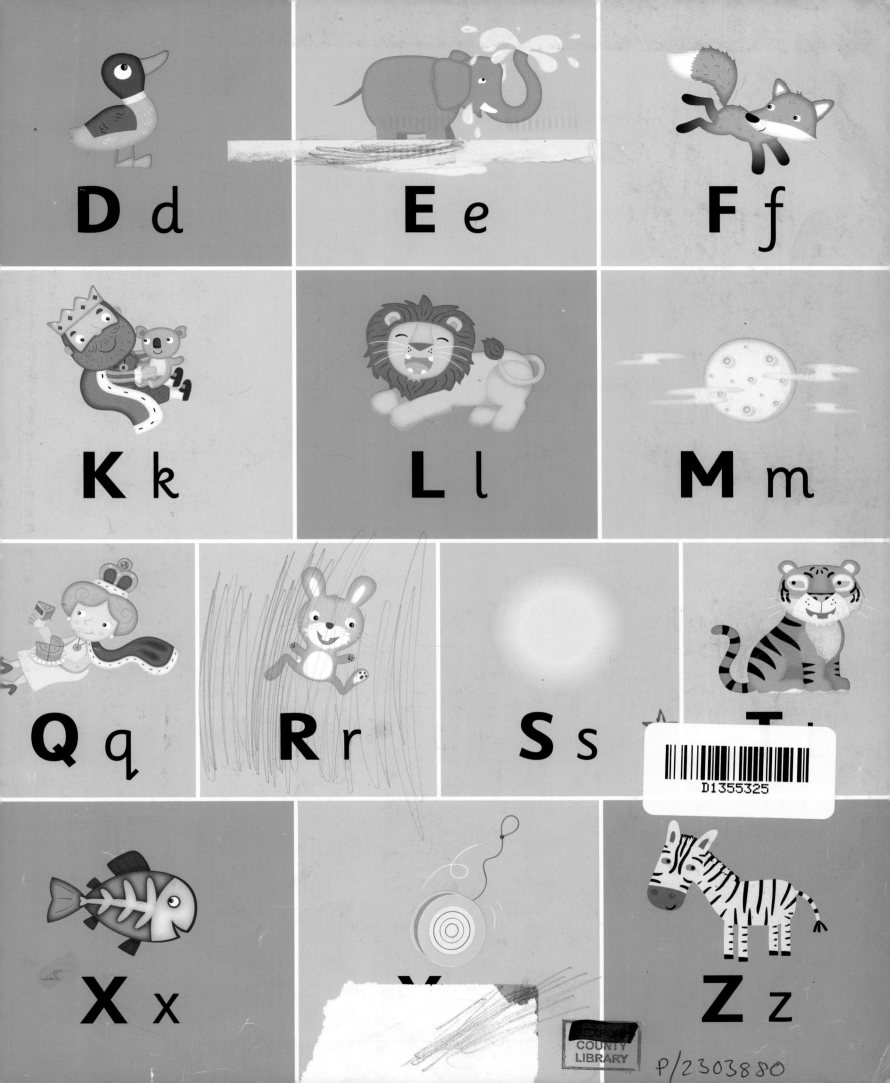

D d

E e

F f

K k

L l

M m

Q q

R r

S s

T t

X x

Z z

Say the Sounds

This is the ideal first book for children who are starting out on their reading journey. It focuses on the sound at the beginning of each word – teachers call this the initial letter sound. Learning these sounds is the first building block to successful reading.

Recognizing these initial letter sounds is a vital step in your child's synthetic phonics learning.

For more advice about phonics and for further activities visit **www.ladybird.com**

What is the difference between A and a?

A is a letter name. Letter names are the letters of the alphabet.

a is a letter sound. Letter sounds are the sounds the letters make.

Here are some words beginning with the **a** sound. Can you say the **a** sound?

arrow

anchor

anteater

angry ant

ambulance

"Atishoo!" sneezed the astronaut.

apple

Adam the alligator found an axe!

axe

Think of some more words that begin with the **a** sound.

Tips on how to use this book with your child:

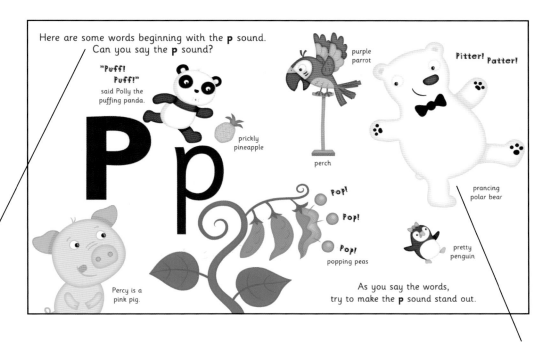

Here are some words beginning with the **p** sound. Can you say the **p** sound?

"Puff! Puff!" said Polly the puffing panda.

prickly pineapple

purple parrot

perch

Pitter! Patter!

prancing polar bear

Pop! Pop! Pop! popping peas

pretty penguin

Percy is a pink pig.

As you say the words, try to make the **p** sound stand out.

Read the simple question to your child and say the sound together.

Have fun pointing to the different pictures on the page. Can your child name them all?

Here are some words beginning with the **s** sound. Can you say the **s** sound?

slippery snail

salad sandwich

spider

S s

seven stars in the sky

sun

Splash! Splash!

Sally is a swimming seal.

six sizzling sausages

Sam sipped his smoothie.

silly seahorse

Slither! Slither!

Simon is a slithering snake.

Think of some more words that begin with the **s** sound.

Using the instructions and questions, encourage your child to have fun with the initial letter sound he can hear.

Make up a story together using the objects and characters on the page. Remember to have fun and don't be afraid of being silly!

Is Simon a dancing snake? No, Simon is a slithering snake. Simon slithers towards six sizzling sausages.

Phonics and educational consultant: Kate Ruttle

Published by Ladybird Books Ltd
A Penguin Company
Penguin Books Ltd, 80 Strand, London WC2R 0RL, UK
Penguin Books Australia Ltd, 707 Collins Street, Melbourne, Victoria 3008, Australia
Penguin Group (NZ) 67 Apollo Drive, Rosedale, North Shore 0632, New Zealand

001

ISBN: 978-0-72327-159-8

Printed in China

Ladybird

I'm Ready... for Phonics!

Say the Sounds

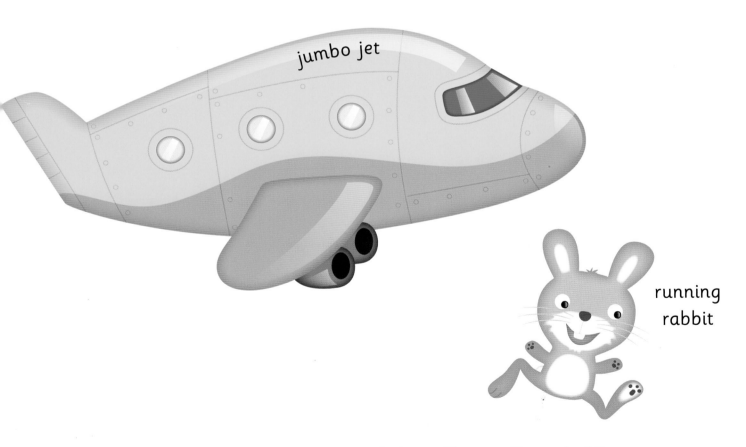

jumbo jet

running rabbit

Illustrated by Ian Cunliffe

Here are some words beginning with the **a** sound. Can you say the **a** sound?

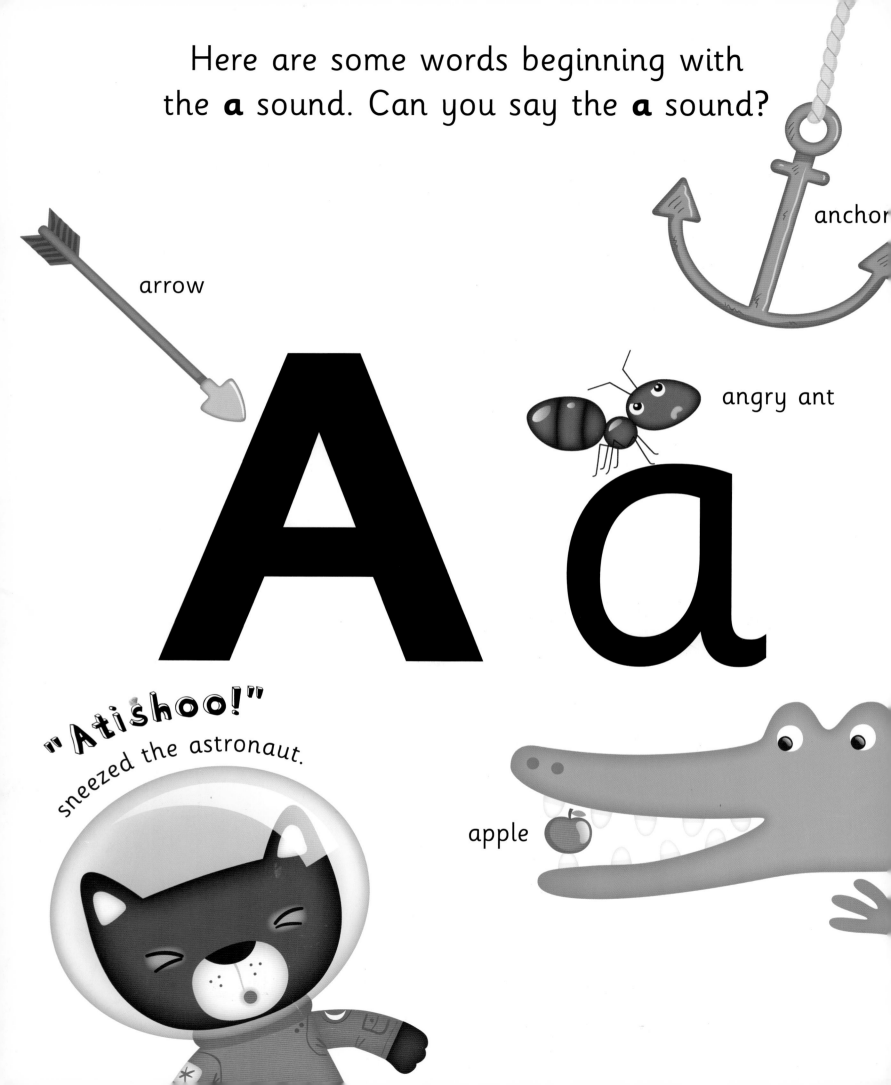

anchor

arrow

angry ant

"Atishoo!"
sneezed the astronaut.

apple

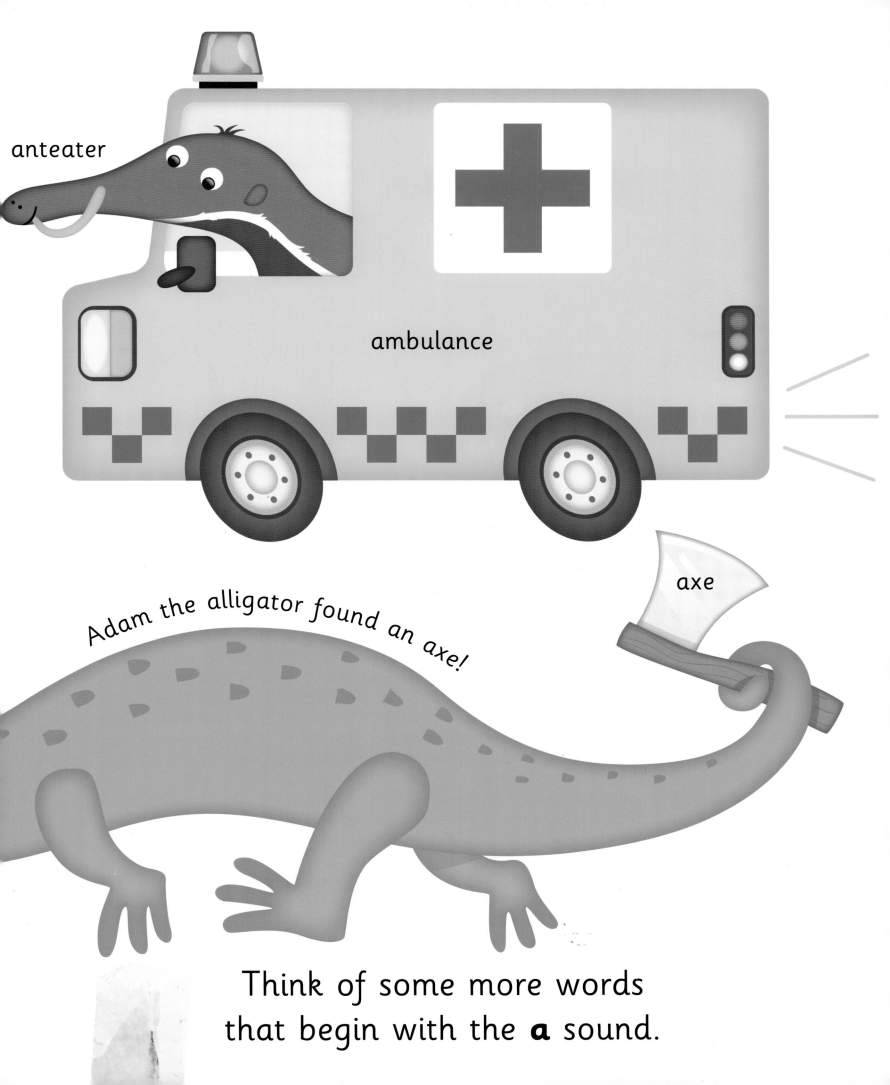

anteater

ambulance

axe

Adam the alligator found an axe!

Think of some more words
that begin with the **a** sound.

Here are some words beginning with the **b** sound.
Can you say the **b** sound?

Brring! Brring!

Ben's brand new bike

bouncy ball

B b

blue bat

Buzz! Buzz!

busy bee

Beep! Beep!

Bob the bat has a boat.

beautiful bird

Bang!

blue balloon

big brown bear

Betty the bear has a bus.

Brrmm! Brrmm!

Count all the animals beginning
with **b** on the page.

Here are some words beginning with the **c** sound.
Can you say the **c** sound?

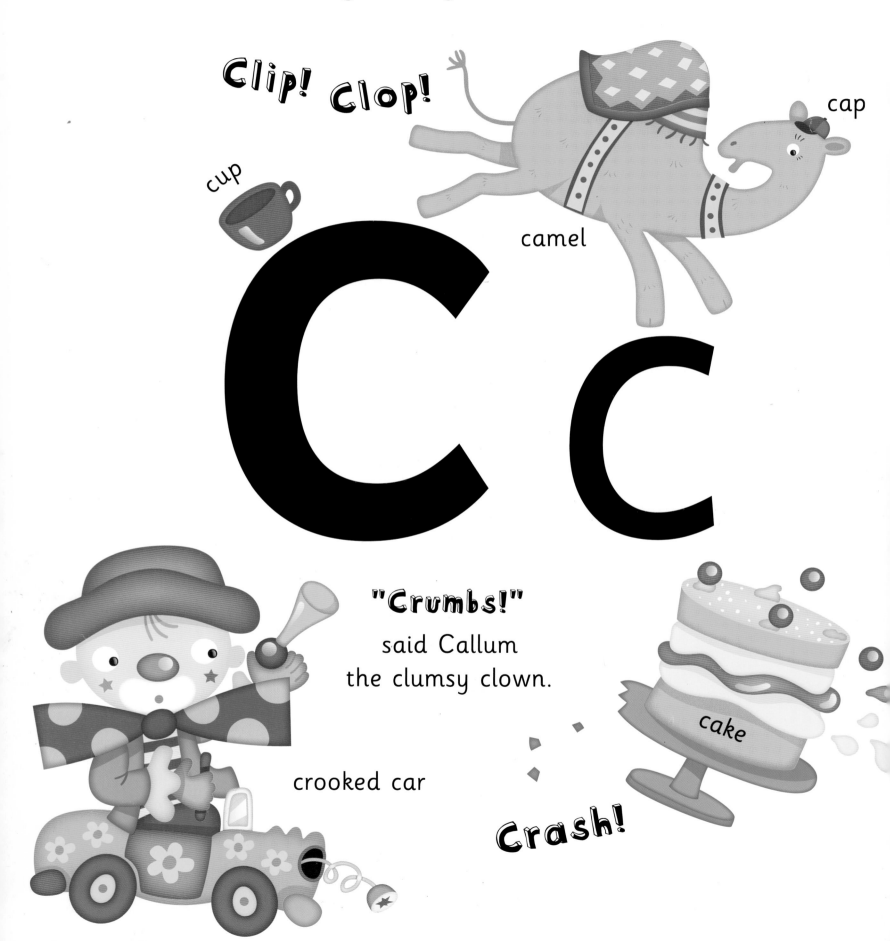

Clip! Clop!

cup

cap

camel

C c

"Crumbs!"
said Callum
the clumsy clown.

crooked car

cake

Crash!

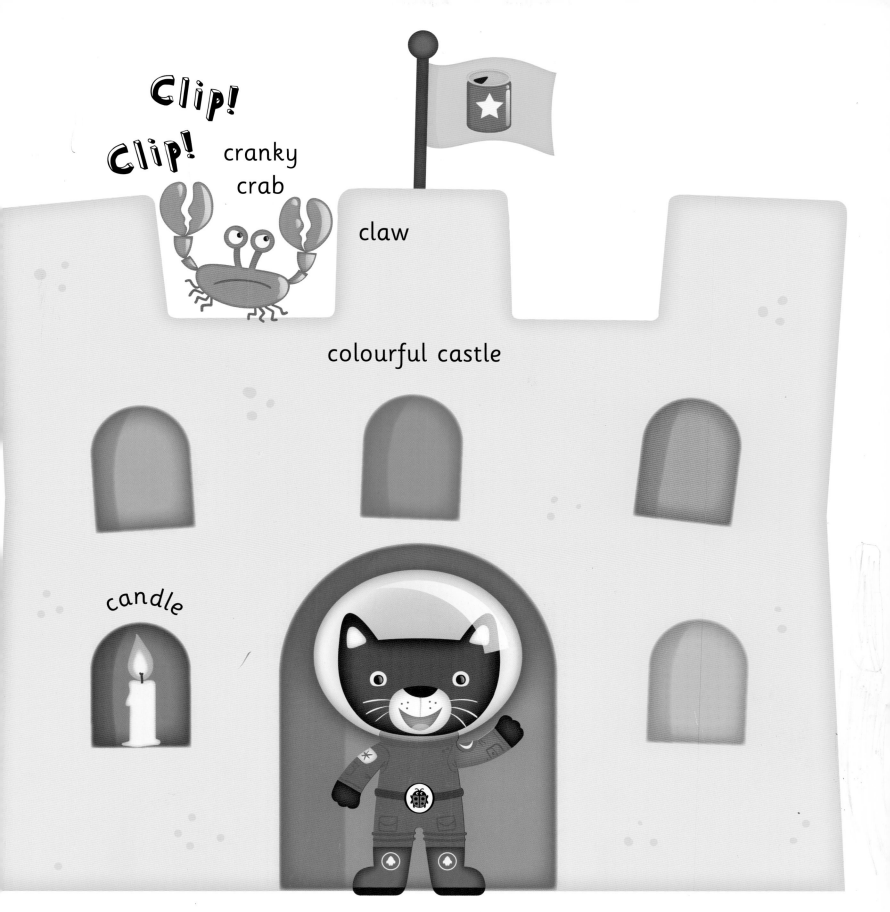

Clip! Clip! cranky crab

claw

colourful castle

candle

Captain Comet is a cat.

As you say the words,
try to make the **c** sound stand out.

Here are some words beginning with the **d** sound.
Can you say the **d** sound?

delighted
dinosaur

diving
dolphin

dotty
dice

duck

D d

Dan the donkey
throws a dart.

Doink!

dartboard

Ding!
Dong!

door

Dad has a
dusty drill.

Daisy the doll rings
the doorbell.

dancing
dog

dangerous
dragon

Think of some more words
that begin with the **d** sound.

Here are some words beginning with the **e** sound.
Can you say the **e** sound?

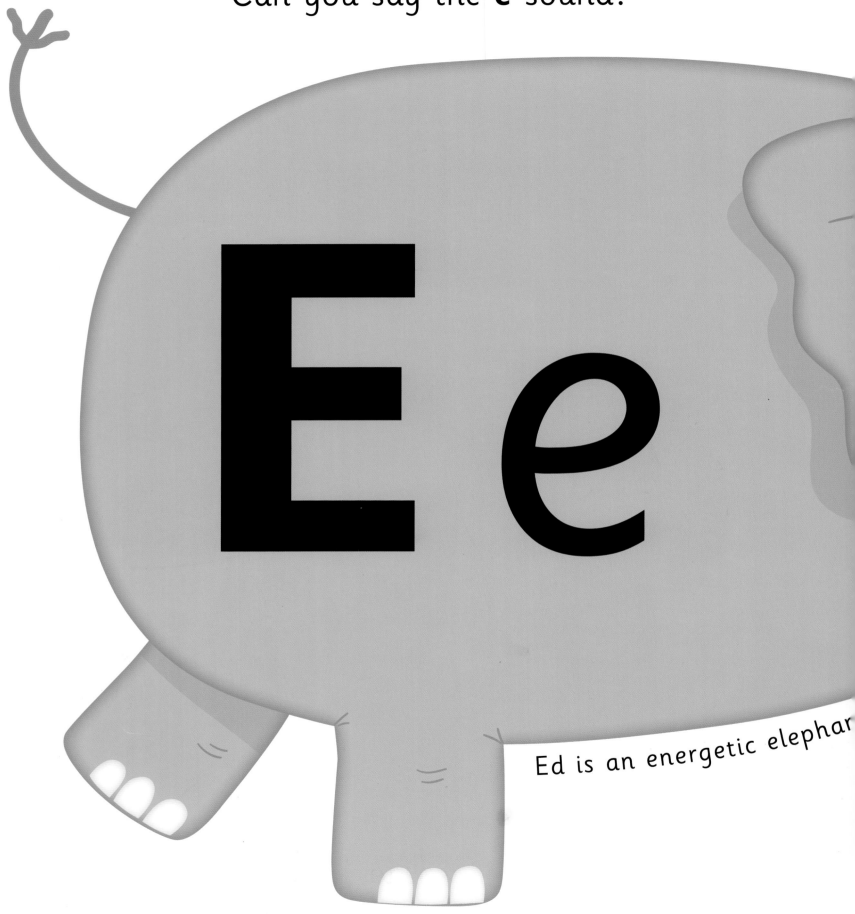

E e

Ed is an energetic elephant

emerald

emperor

empty envelope

Ellie the elf
is excited.

elegant
egg

As you say the words,
try to make the **e** sound stand out.

Here are some words beginning with the **f** sound. Can you say the **f** sound?

Fizz! Fizz!

four fabulous fireworks

F f

fork

Fred the farmer chased the fox with a fork.

fence

fox

Flutter!

Flutter!

fancy butterfly

feathers

funny flamingo

As you say the words,
try to make the **f** sound stand out.

Here are some words beginning with the **g** sound. Can you say the **g** sound?

greedy grey goat

"Grr! Grr!" grumbled the grumpy gorilla.

grap

golden goose

Gita gave Grace a gift.

green grass

"Growl! Growl!"
grizzled Gordon
the grizzly bear.

Gurgle!
Gurgle!"
giggled the
baby girl.

guitar

Count all the animals beginning
with **g** on the page.

Here are some words beginning with the **h** sound.
Can you say the **h** sound?

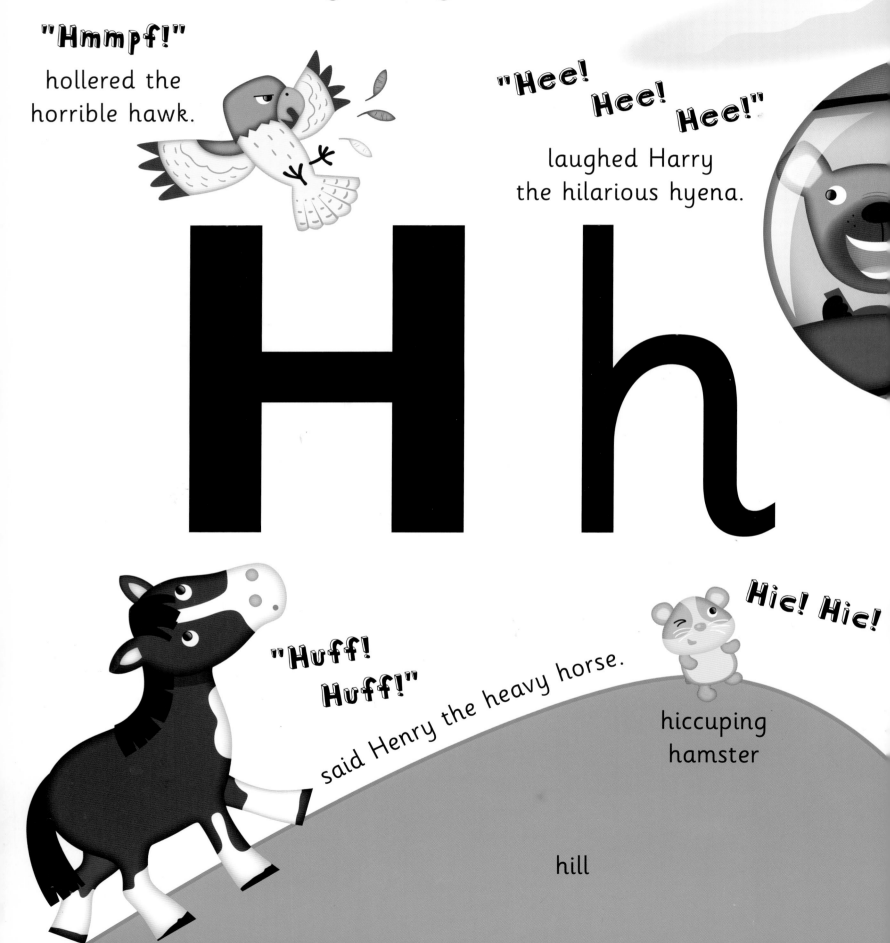

"Hmmpf!"

hollered the
horrible hawk.

"Hee!
Hee!
Hee!"

laughed Harry
the hilarious hyena.

H h

"Huff!
Huff!"

said Henry the heavy horse.

Hic! Hic!

hiccuping
hamster

hill

helicopter

happy hen

henhouse

Hester is a hairy hippo.

Think of some more words that begin with the **h** sound.

Here are some words beginning with the i sound.
Can you say the i sound?

intelligent
iguana

What an interesting igloo!

Ii

itchy
insects

Izzy is inside
the igloo.

ink

As you say the words,
try to make the i sound stand out

Here are some words beginning with the **j** sound.
Can you say the **j** sound?

jumbo jet

John is a
jolly juggler.

J j

Jump!
Jump!

jiggling jellyfish

jumping
Jack-in-the-box

Think of some more words
that begin with the **j** sound.

Here are some words beginning with the **k** sound.
Can you say the **k** sound?

kite

kind king

koala

kicking
kangaroo

keys

As you say the words,
try to make the **k** sound stand out.

Here are some words beginning with the l sound
Can you say the l sound?

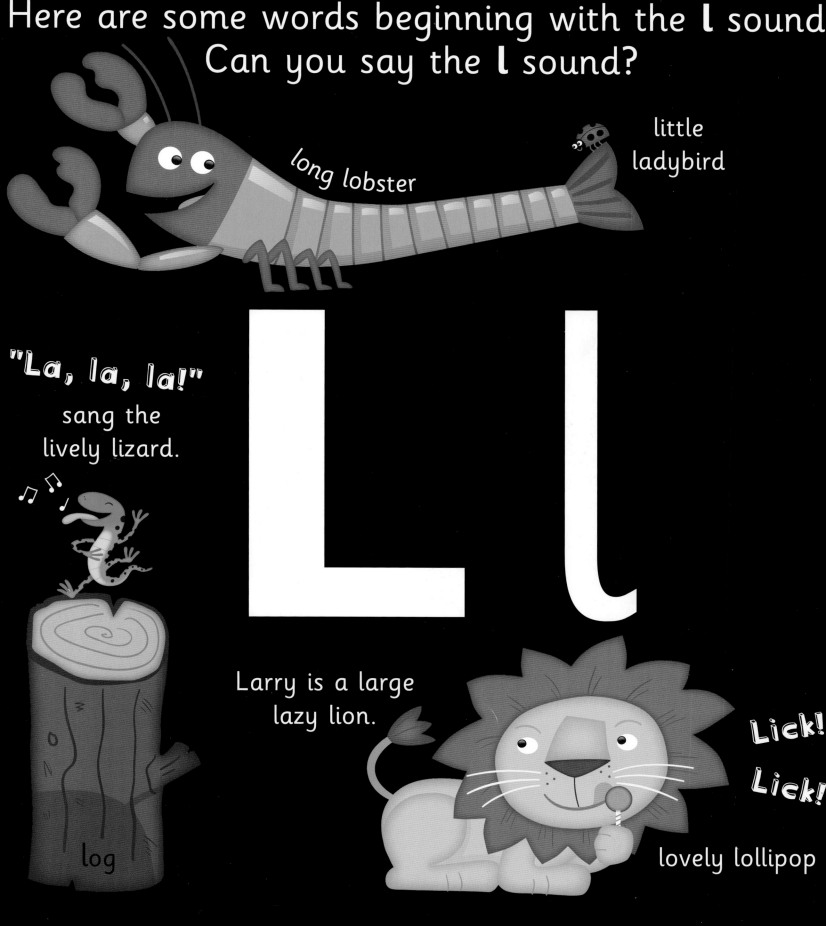

long lobster

little
ladybird

"La, la, la!"
sang the
lively lizard.

log

Larry is a large
lazy lion.

Lick!
Lick!

lovely lollipop

Think of some more words
that begin with the l sound.

Here are some words beginning with the **m** sound
Can you say the **m** sound?

misty moon

magic mirror

marvellous magician

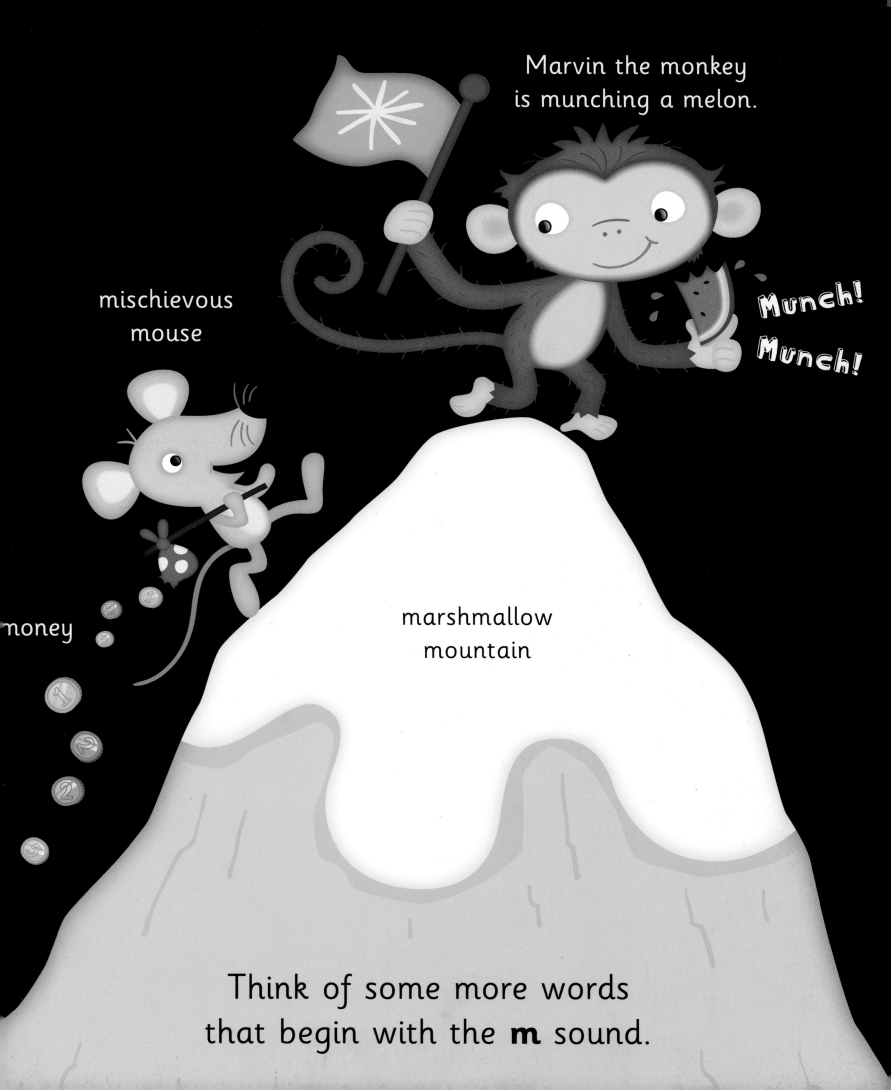

Marvin the monkey
is munching a melon.

mischievous
mouse

Munch!
Munch!

money

marshmallow
mountain

Think of some more words
that begin with the **m** sound.

Here are some words beginning with the **n** sound. Can you say the **n** sound?

"Neigh!"

neighed Nora the nag.

net

Nip! Nip!

Ned is a nipping newt.

nest

Nn

nine nosy neighbours

As you say the words, try to make the **n** sound stand out.

Here are some words beginning with the **o** sound.
Can you say the **o** sound?

octopus

ostrich

O o

odd
otter

oranges

ox

oblong

Count all the animals beginning
with **o** on the page.

Here are some words beginning with the **p** sound. Can you say the **p** sound?

"Puff! Puff!" said Polly the puffing panda.

prickly pineapple

Percy is a pink pig.

purple
parrot

Pitter! Patter!

perch

Pop!

Pop!

Pop!

popping peas

prancing
polar bear

pretty
penguin

As you say the words,
try to make the **p** sound stand out.

Here are some words beginning with the **q** sound.
Can you say the **q** sound?

quilt

quiet queen

quarter

"Quack! Quack!"
quacked the ducks.

As you say the words,
try to make the **q** sound stand out.

Here are some words beginning with the **r** sound.
Can you say the **r** sound?

Rattle! Rattle!

red racing robots

R r

running
rabbit

rat

rainbow

roaring rocket

"Ribbit! Ribbit!"
said the frog.

Think of some more words
that begin with the **r** sound.

Here are some words beginning with the **s** sound. Can you say the **s** sound?

slippery
snail

salad
sandwich

spider

S s

silly
seahorse

Sam sipped
his smoothie.

seven stars
in the sky

sun

Splash!
Splash!

Sally is a
swimming seal.

six sizzling
sausages

Slither!
Slither!

Simon is a
slithering snake.

Think of some more words
that begin with the **s** sound.

Here are some words beginning with the **t** sound. Can you say the **t** sound?

Tickle! Tickle!

terrific tortoise

turquoise teddy

tomatoes

ten tiny tractors

"**Tut! Tut!**"
tutted Tina
the tiger.

"**Tweet! Tweet!**"
twittered two turtle doves.

fle

teapot

tea

Tick!

Tock!

tail

toast

ticking
clock

table

toad

As you say the words,
try to make the **t** sound stand out.

Here are some words beginning with the **u** sound.
Can you say the **u** sound?

Up! Up! Up!

upside-down umbrella

"Uh-oh!"
said Uncle.

Uncle's ugly
underwear

As you say the words,
try to make the **u** sound stand out.

Here are some words beginning with the **v** sound. Can you say the **v** sound?

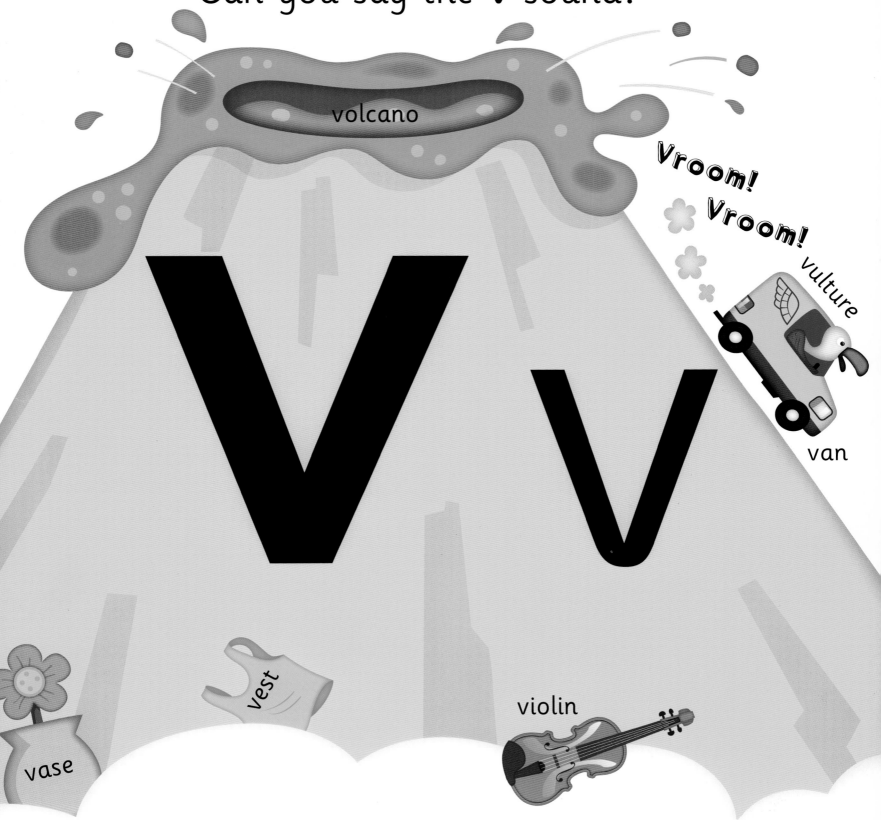

volcano

Vroom! Vroom!

vulture

van

vest

violin

vase

Think of some more words that begin with the **v** sound.

Here are some words beginning with the **w** sound. Can you say the **w** sound?

wicked witch

"Woo! Woo!"

wailed Wendy the wolf.

Walter is a wet walrus.

wiggly worm

Count all the animals beginning with **w** on the page.

Here are some words beginning with **x**.

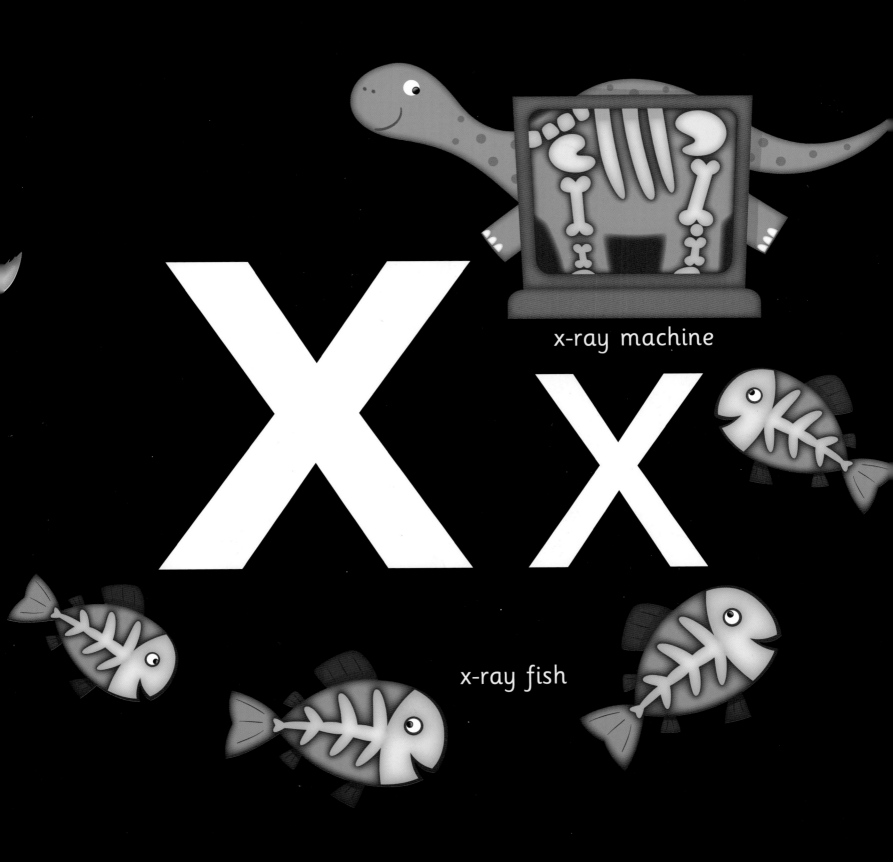

x-ray machine

x-ray fish

When you say the words, try to make
the **x** at the front of the word stand out.

Here are some words beginning with the **y** sound.
Can you say the **y** sound?

Yawn!
Yawn!

yawning
yak

Y y

"yes!"
yelled Yan.

yummy
yoghurt

yellow yo-yo

Think of some more words
that begin with the **y** sound.

Here are some words beginning with the **z** sound.
Can you say the **z** sound?

Zoom! Zoom!

zip

Z z

Zzz!
Zzz!

Zelda the
sleepy zebra.

zombie

zig-zagging zoo car

zoo keeper

As you say the words,
try to make the **z** sound stand out.

A a

B b

C c

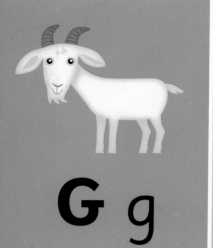

G g

H h

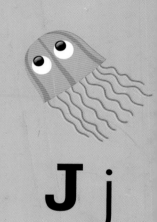

I i

J j

N n

O o

P p

U u

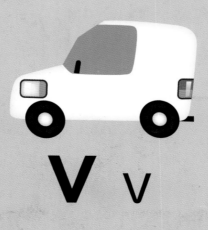

V v

W w